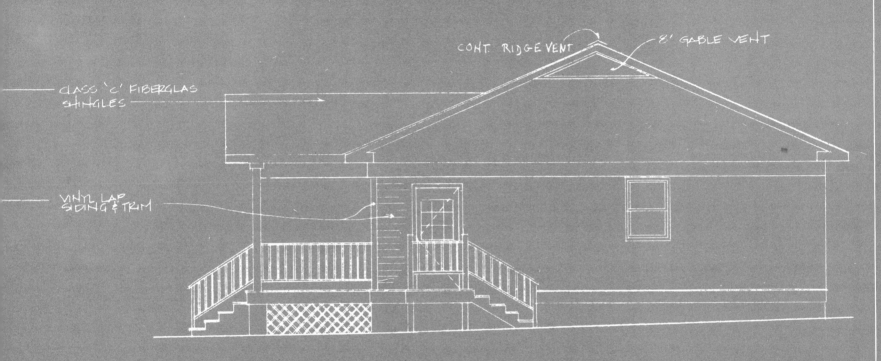

CONT. RIDGE VENT

8' GABLE VENT

CLASS 'C' FIBERGLAS SHINGLES

VINYL LAP SIDING & TRIM

CMU FOUNDATION

RIGHT SIDE ELEVATION 3 BEDROOM

The President Builds
a House

The President Builds a House

TEXT BY Tom Shachtman

PHOTOGRAPHS BY Margaret Miller

INTRODUCTION BY Jimmy Carter

SIMON AND SCHUSTER BOOKS FOR YOUNG READERS
Published by Simon and Schuster Inc., New York

SIMON AND SCHUSTER
BOOKS FOR YOUNG READERS
Simon & Schuster Building
Rockefeller Center
1230 Avenue of the Americas
New York, New York 10020

Text Copyright © 1989 by Tom Shachtman
Photographs Copyright © 1989 by Margaret Miller
All rights reserved
including the right of reproduction
in whole or in part in any form.

SIMON AND SCHUSTER BOOKS FOR YOUNG READERS
is a trademark of Simon & Schuster Inc.·

Designed by Kathleen Westray
Manufactured in the United States of America

10 9 8 7 6 5 4 3 2

Library of Congress Cataloging in Publication Data

Shachtman, Tom, 1942–
The president builds a house: the work of habitat for humanity
by Tom Shachtman; photographs by Margaret Miller;
introduction by Jimmy Carter.
p.   cm.
Summary: A photo essay depicts the non-profit organization of
volunteers that renovate or build houses for needy families as,
with former President and Mrs. Jimmy Carter's participation as
volunteers, they build twenty houses in Atlanta in just five days.
1. Poor—Housing—Georgia—Atlanta—Pictorial works—Juvenile
literature.   2. Habitat for Humanity, inc.—Pictorial works—Juvenile
literature.   [1. Poor—Housing—Georgia—Atlanta.   2. Habitat
for Humanity, inc.]   I. Miller, Margaret, 1945– ill. II. Title.
HD7287.96.U62A867   1989
386.5′8—dc19   88-33267
                              CIP

ISBN 0-671-67705-5

To Alan Benjamin
who fathered this book,
and to all the dedicated volunteers
of Habitat for Humanity
T. S. and M. M.

INTRODUCTION

All of us—children as well as parents and grand-parents—believe there are many things wrong with our world. Poverty and particularly the lack of good housing and homelessness are conditions that seriously affect many families. We often feel these problems are so large that we as individuals can't do anything about them—but that isn't so. Habitat for Humanity has shown us that when people get together in a caring and cooperative way, wonderful things can be accomplished. Following lessons from the Bible that tell us to house the poor and to lend money without interest, Habitat for Humanity builds houses with and for poor families that they wouldn't be able to afford otherwise.

My wife, Rosalynn, and I have been involved with Habitat for Humanity since 1982, as volunteer homebuilders and as directors of the organization. It is one of the most exciting and gratifying experiences we have had since leaving the White House.

In this book, you'll learn about Habitat for Humanity and about a week we spent with several hundred other volunteers in Atlanta, Georgia, building twenty new homes for twenty wonderful families who worked beside us. Because of Habitat, these families now have not only new homes but also new outlooks on life.

My hope is that this book, like Habitat for Humanity itself, may encourage people of all ages and all faiths to reach out to help others, knowing that their efforts *can* make a difference.

Jimmy Carter

One hot week in June, Mayor Andrew Young welcomes hundreds of Habitat for Humanity volunteers to Atlanta. Their goal: to erect a neighborhood in five days, homes for twenty families, most of whom have never before lived in a decent place they could call their own.

Mayor Young and other concerned people speak of an era of homelessness in America. This reminds everyone of the importance of what will be done here. Five to ten thousand people in Atlanta have no homes, and one quarter of the city's housing is below standards for minimum health, safety and comfort. In America as a whole, there may be two million homeless people, twenty million in substandard housing.

Many people who live in inadequate homes drift away from their small town roots and move to big cities where rents are high. All too often, their lives become caught up in an unending cycle of poverty and despair. Building one group of twenty homes can't change all that, of course; but the Habitat project is to be a demonstration of what can be done—if people will work for change.

Seeing just the foundations and
building materials, the volunteers
wonder: will they be able to do it?

Work begins. The volunteers toil alongside members of the families who are to own the homes when they are completed. All workers are divided into teams, each with a team captain. About one third of the volunteers have done this sort of work before; another third are familiar with it—home carpenters. Together they help the rest, who have never done any building before.

The air fills with the drumbeats of many hammers.

Nearly every task is a matter of cooperation:
One person to hold, the other to hammer.
One to hand up, the other to put in place.
One to sweep, the other to wield the dustpan.
Two to carry a bulky load.

Where there's a will…

...there's soon a wall.

The workers are joined by their common faith and by a common task.
Mistakes are made; but a badly hammered nail can be pulled out,
a wrongly measured line can be redrawn.

By Monday evening the structural skeletons of the homes are complete. Everyone is tired—and happy.

The next day, after the "outlines"
of the houses are completed,
the "details" can be filled in.

Each window must be hung and fitted with care.

Roofs are attached and shingled. Workers who never thought they could stand atop a building manage to do so.

The houses will be warm in winter and cool in summer after insulation is stuffed inside the walls.

By Tuesday afternoon Jimmy Carter decides he can't stay in his office any longer and comes out to work, eager to begin. The former president wasn't expected until Wednesday. He is Habitat's most famous volunteer...and an energetic worker, too.

A carpenter and woodworker in his spare time, Mr. Carter is comfortable when at work with his hands. For him, work on Habitat projects is part recreation…and part dedication to the cause.

As with other volunteers, President Carter was drawn to the work of Habitat for Humanity by the ideas, enthusiasm and religious faith of Habitat's founder, Millard Fuller.

Back in 1965 Millard Fuller was a young lawyer whose mail-order business had already made him a millionaire. But pursuing his fortune had caused his personal life to become a shambles. He and his wife, Linda, decided to give away everything they owned, and to dedicate their lives to Christian causes. While working at a Christian community in south Georgia, and later in Africa as a missionary, Millard saw that with effort and faith, much could be done to house the world's poor.

"No more shacks!" he vowed. If poor families had decent homes, he believed, they would be able to make better lives for themselves.

The Bible teaches that:

We are our brothers' keepers.
We must help those who are less fortunate.
We should loan money and not charge interest.

Millard Fuller made these principles the basis of Habitat for Humanity, the organization he began in 1976.

Millard translated these principles into Habitat's guiding ideas:

We must help our neighbors by building houses with them that they might otherwise never obtain. Each home's cost must be kept low through donations of money, materials and labor. All homes must be paid for over a period of years by the families—the homes are not gifts, for Habitat is not a charity that gives things away. But Habitat will not demand interest as a part of the mortgage payments. Millard calls the no-interest provision "Biblical economics," since the idea of lending money but not charging interest is mentioned in the Bible. Every family who will own one of Habitat's homes must work many hours alongside volunteers. This notion is often called "sweat equity."

Starting modestly in the small town of Americus, Georgia, the Habitat idea and way of helping people obtain shelter has become a worldwide movement.

There are Habitat projects in many developing nations—in South America, Africa, even in far-away Papua New Guinea—and in hundreds of cities in the United States and other industrial nations. What Millard calls "poverty housing" is bad housing and must be replaced, whether it's a run-down tenement in New York City or a grass-and-mud hut in Guatemala.

On Wednesday President Carter and former First Lady Rosalynn Carter make their first formal appearance at the site.

"It's very important to reach out to those who are not like us, especially to those who are less fortunate than we," says the president during an informal press conference. It is a lesson he often teaches in Sunday school, and which he feels he is putting into practice through his work with Habitat.

The Carters greet old friends with whom they have worked on other Habitat projects, and get to know some of the families who will live in these new homes.

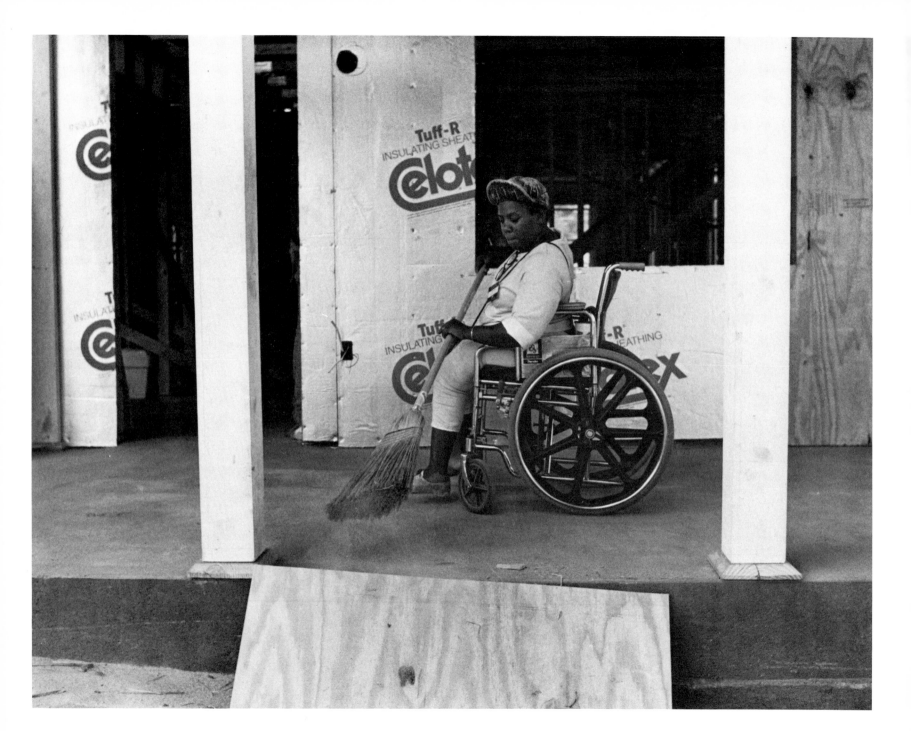

The president meets the owner-to-be of the house on which he is assigned to work. She is Jackie Gray, a wheelchair-bound single mother. Mr. Carter admires her efforts to work just as hard on her new home as any other volunteer. "She's tireless," he says.

Most of the people who are to own the houses in this Habitat effort previously lived in the area, in run-down, cramped places, sleeping three and four to a room. They are usually described as "the working poor"—people who are employed but who don't earn enough money to buy a good home. One family was previously homeless. All the families have children —that's one of the requirements for a family to be eligible for a Habitat home in this location. Some are single-mother families; one has a single father. Others will have several generations living under one roof.

The Askews are typical of the families chosen by Habitat. Jeffrey is a sanitation worker; his wife, Angela, serves food in a school cafeteria. They've already decided that their two boys will share a room and that their new baby—expected shortly— will have a room of his or her own.

There are thousands of tasks to be done in building a new home. The process usually takes several weeks or months—but these homes must go up in five days. Supply trucks are ready with ten different kinds of nails, miles of insulation, enough paint to fill a swimming pool, electrical sockets, linoleum for the floors, latticework wood for handsome porches, and more.

Behind every hand that hefts a hammer on the Habitat project are several more hands that feed, lodge and care for the volunteers, and that contribute materials to the project. The estimated value of the donations from four hundred suppliers is $350,000.

For several months before the arrival of the workers, hundreds of local volunteers (as well as the families who will live in the homes) spent thousands of hours preparing the sites, gathering materials and loading them onto trucks so they could be used in the proper order.

The work, though arduous, is fun. "We get as much out of it as we put into it," President Carter says. People work very well—and cheerfully—when they work with a clear and distinct sense of purpose.

This is the way friendships grow.
This the way laughter begins.
This is the way we manage to do tasks that
two days ago we thought we'd never be able
to accomplish.

At lunchtime the workers are served by volunteers from various local church and civic organizations. One group of children drew happy scenes on the lunch bags they packed. During this week, all breakfasts, lunches and dinners are donated and served by local volunteers. Their support is part of the vast organizational effort that enables the workers to finish the task of building twenty homes in a week.

During this building week, volunteers administer first aid, tend the supply trucks and the refreshment tents, take care of security, and do many other tasks to make the building process go more smoothly.

Why would people give up their vacation time and spend their own money to come here from all over the country and from foreign lands to help build houses—homes they will never live in?

For Dale Young, from Westchester, New York, it's an emotional experience to see at firsthand how her own work will help others. "Most people take their comfortable homes for granted," she points out. "When you ask suburban children what they're thankful for, they seldom mention their homes. They find it hard to imagine what life would be like without a bed or a room or a roof to call their own."

Willie Wilkerson, a Vietnam veteran and a teacher of building trades in an Atlanta high school, knows what that difference is. The families who will own these homes, he tells author Tom Shachtman, have been set limits by society; they're "victims of the kicking machine. All too often they've been told 'no' and 'you can't do this.' Now we're going to help them have a base. We're saying 'yes' to them."

"Having a home," says Mr. Wilkerson, "will encourage them to go forward with a belief that they *can* get somewhere—push for a promotion, study for a degree, make an investment. It's very important that these houses are going to families with children."

During a break from work, President Carter explains in an interview his interest in Habitat by referring to the Bible. "Jesus was a carpenter," he says. "He worked alongside Joseph to provide housing for the people of Nazareth—permanent things. Habitat is an opportunity to pattern part of our lives after His, to uphold such important values as trust, beauty, service and friendship."

Conversations about spiritual matters often spring up among the volunteers. Many have come to this Habitat project to demonstrate their beliefs; and they find that while doing "the Lord's work," they are more easily able to discuss deeply felt convictions they might not talk about in more everyday settings.

As Millard Fuller says, "We all ask, 'What is life all about? Why are we here? In the context of eternity, how ought we to spend our time?'" The answer, he says, is "in doing things that go beyond our own self-interest, to help others. When you're immersed in the work to the point that you stop thinking about yourself, then you find true meaning."

As he walks through the site, or when he speaks in front of groups in the many cities to which he travels, Mr. Fuller thanks people for their involvement—and challenges them to do more. He reminds them that when the Civil Rights Movement pushed America to see equal rights for every citizen as a matter of conscience, we moved toward a more equitable, integrated society.

Millard Fuller wants Habitat to be a housing conscience for the world, to create a climate in everyone's mind in which "poverty housing and homelessness are not tolerated by our society."

Jeff Carter, one of the president's children, joins his parents in working with Habitat. A computer scientist and entrepreneur, he's thinking about asking his entire office force to come to work on future projects.

The work continues. Many volunteers are learning, in detail, what it takes to build a house. Behind the insulation in a wall there must be electrical wiring and water pipes. A floor is not complete without a covering of linoleum, carpeting or wood finish. And a house may seem unfinished without kitchen appliances, landscaping, and other touches to transform it into a "livable" home.

Ola Stephens, whose family will occupy one of the homes, is a divorced single mother whose daily job is pouring concrete for public construction sites, such as highways and viaducts. Her mother, who will also live in the house, is ill and can no longer work. Ola has four children. Early one hot morning, her children come to see what will be their new home. Children from many of the other families are also brought to the still-unfinished houses later in the day, after most of the work has been done. All are excited about picking out bedrooms, thinking about building a barbecue in the backyard or plotting out a garden.

Because Ola will pay less each month to own this home than she was paying for a small apartment, she plans to put aside some of the money toward college educations for her children.

Now they'll have room…to dream.

As the week nears an end, some crews work far into the night or arrive early in the morning to get everything done before the deadline.

The houses are finished! One after another, the volunteers step back and look
at their work. All who were involved feel a sense of accomplishment, of pride
at what can be done by people who are willing to work for a goal.

How can we leave tomorrow and never see our new friends again? The volunteers exchange phone numbers and addresses, promising to keep in touch. They make plans to meet at another Habitat project—perhaps next year at one in Milwaukee or, the year after that, in Tijuana, Mexico. As Habitat veterans know, after volunteers return to their homes, many will discover how much poverty housing exists in their own towns—bad housing that they've lived near but have never truly "seen" before. The hope is that they and their friends and neighbors will start Habitat projects in their own towns.

When that happens, this week-long project will have fulfilled a major promise: to be *a model for what can be done* in every community that needs to replace poverty housing. This year Habitat's many local groups will build two thousand homes. Next year they aim to erect four thousand. Habitat's ultimate goal is much more than to build twenty homes; it is to eliminate poverty housing altogether.

As the Carters pose for pictures outside the completed homes, the president suggests to the volunteers: "Come back in a year. You'll see a whole neighborhood that is sparkling clean. No graffiti. No trash. These people will care about their homes. Owning a part of the American dream will also enable them to care more for their community; beyond that, they'll have hope for the future."

On Friday Atlanta Habitat officers give the new homeowners keys to the homes they have helped to build, and ask them to sign legal documents. All of the money from the mortgage payments the homeowners will send to Habitat each month will be "recycled"— it will be used to build still more houses for needy people across this country and around the world.

JIMMY CARTER
WORK PROJECT '88
JACQUELINE
Gray

HABITAT FOR HUMANITY

The ceremony is emotional both for the volunteers and for the new homeowners. Many are moved to tears. "These homes have been made with love," says Millard Fuller," and we know that you'll treat them with love. For you are signing more than a legal contract with Habitat. You are entering into a spiritual covenant, becoming part of the worldwide Habitat community."

By wisdom a house is built, and by understanding it is established; by knowledge the rooms are filled with all precious and pleasant riches.   Proverbs 24:3–4.

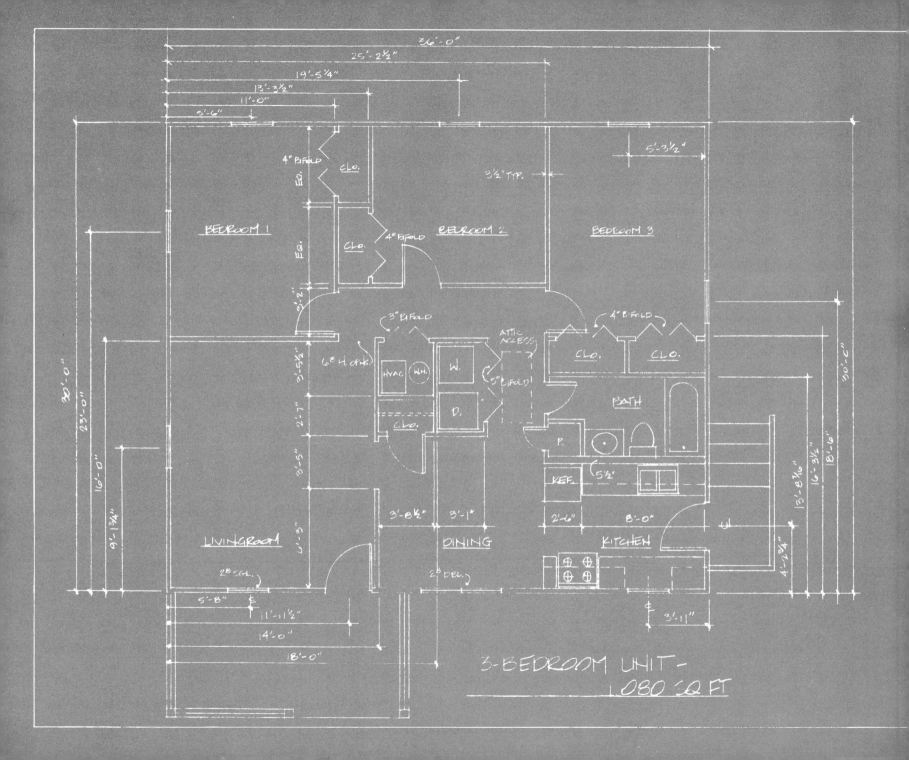

3-BEDROOM UNIT -
1,080 SQ FT